The Badger

Copyright © by Harcourt, Inc.

All rights reserved. No part of this publication may be reproduced or transmitted in any form or by any means, electronic or mechanical, including photocopy, recording, or any information storage and retrieval system, without permission in writing from the publisher.

Requests for permission to make copies of any part of the work should be addressed to School Permissions and Copyrights, Harcourt, Inc., 6277 Sea Harbor Drive, Orlando, Florida 32887-6777. Fax 407-345-2418.

HARCOURT and the Harcourt Logo are trademarks of Harcourt, Inc., registered in the United States of America and/or other jurisdictions.
Printed in the United States of America

ISBN 10: 0-15-367255-2   ISBN 13: 978-0-15-367255-2

3 4 5 6 7 8 9 10 179 10 09 08

If you have received these materials as examination copies free of charge, Harcourt School Publishers retains title to the materials and they may not be resold. Resale of examination copies is strictly prohibited and is illegal.

Possession of this publication in print format does not entitle users to convert this publication, or any portion of it, into electronic format.

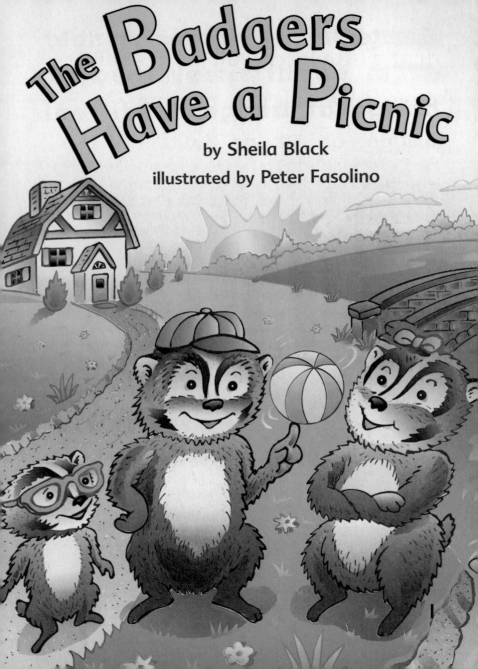

The Badgers Have a Picnic

by Sheila Black

illustrated by Peter Fasolino

"Let's have a picnic!" said
Greg. "We'll sit by the
bridge at Dodge Lake."

"I'll help," said Madge.
Greg sniffed. "You're much
too little to help."

"I'll pack ginger snaps and this large wedge of fudge," said Ginny.

4

"We'll get sick if we eat just that," said Greg. "I'll pack oranges and sandwiches."

5

"We forgot something,"
Ginny said.
"Is it this wedge of
cheese?" asked Greg.

"No, we need the basket,"
Madge said. "I can reach it."

Madge smiled a big, big
smile. "Here it is!" she
said. "See? I told you
I could help!"